ALiCE'S ADVENTURES in WONDERLAND

A COLOURING BOOK

WITH THE ORIGINAL ILLUSTRATIONS BY
SIR JOHN TENNIEL

Down, down, down. Would the fall never come to an end? "I wonder how many miles I've fallen by this time?" she said aloud.

... The Rabbit actually took a watch out of its waistcoat-pocket, and looked at it...

The Rabbit started violently, dropped the white kid-gloves and the fan, and scurried away into the darkness as hard as he could go.

. . . She came upon a low curtain she
had not noticed before and behind it was
a little door about fifteen inches high:

She went on growing, and growing...

…After waiting till she fancied she heard the Rabbit just under the window, she suddenly spread out her hand, and made a snatch in the air.

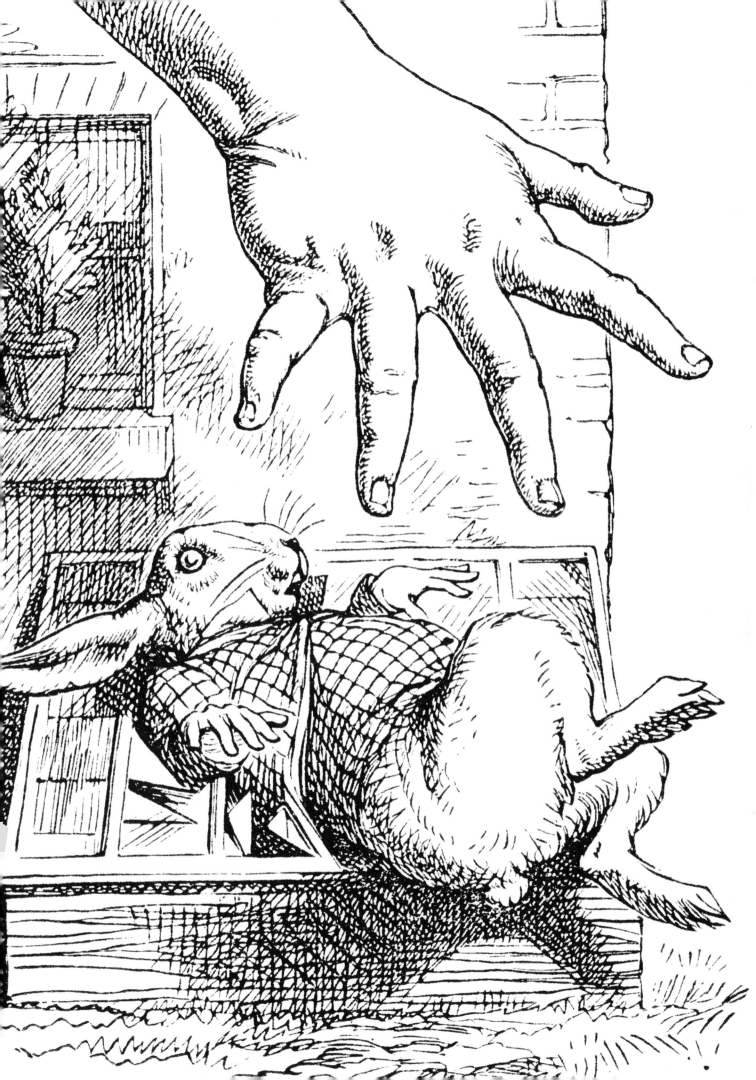

... Tied round the neck of the bottle was a paper label, with the words "*DRINK ME*" beautifully printed on it in large letters.

At last the Mouse, who seemed to be a person of some authority among them, called out "Sit down, all of you, and listen to me!"

The chief difficulty Alice found at first was in managing her flamingo...

The first thing
she heard was a
general chorus of
"There goes Bill!"
then the Rabbit's
voice alone—
"Catch him, you
by the hedge!"

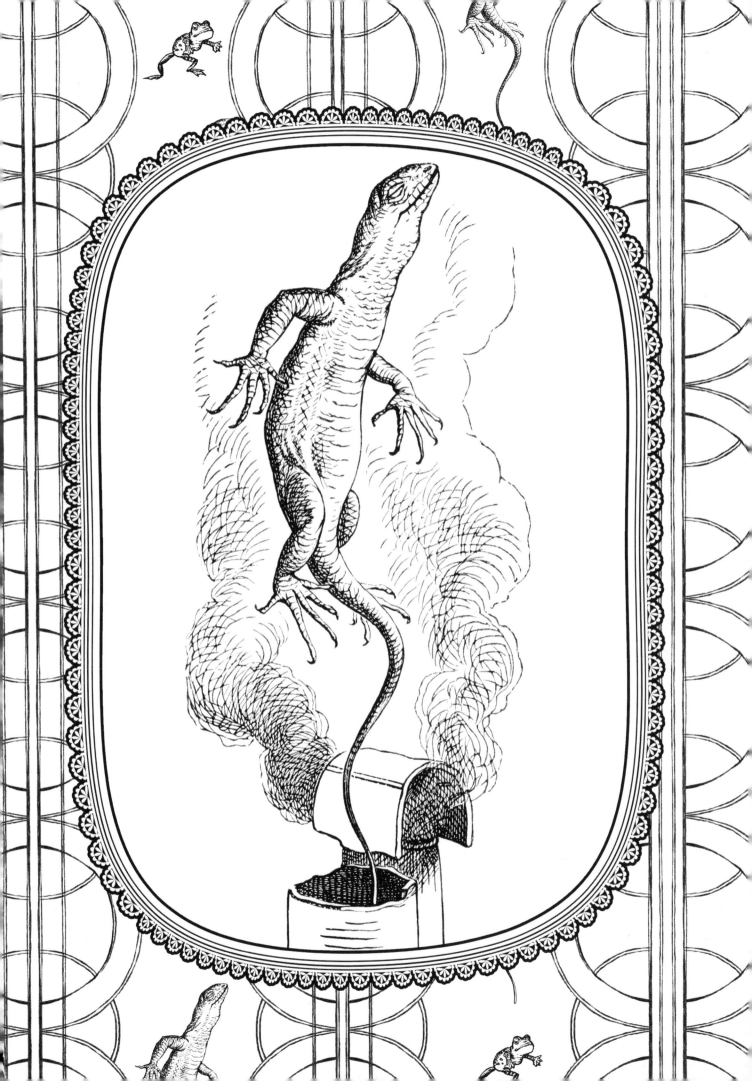

She stretched herself up on tiptoe, and peeped over the edge of the mushroom, and her eyes immediately met those of a large blue caterpillar...

The judge, by the way, was the King;
and, as he wore his crown over the wig,
he did not look at all comfortable.

"You can't think how glad I am to see you again, you dear old thing!" said the Duchess, as she tucked her arm affectionately into Alice's...

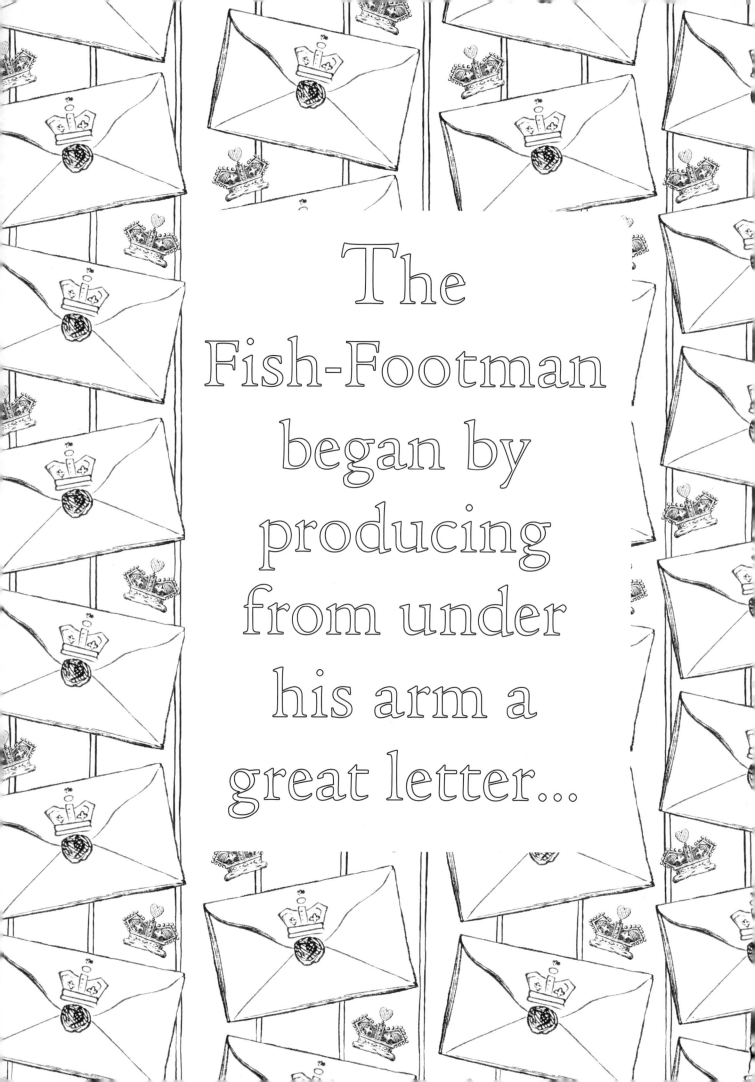

The
Fish-Footman
began by
producing
from under
his arm a
great letter...

Then they all crowded round her once more, while the Dodo solemnly presented the thimble, saying, "We beg your acceptance of this elegant thimble";

When she got back to the Cheshire-Cat, she was surprised to find quite a large crowd collected round it:

"*Twinkle, twinkle,* little bat! How I wonder what you're at! You know the song, perhaps?"

The Cat only grinned when it saw Alice. It looked good-natured, she thought...

"If it had grown up," she said to herself, "it would have made a dreadfully ugly child: but it makes rather a handsome pig, I think."

The Queen turned crimson with fury, and, after glaring at her for a moment like a wild beast, began screaming, "Off with her head! Off with—"

Alice looked all round the table, but there was nothing on it but tea. "I don't see any wine," she remarked.

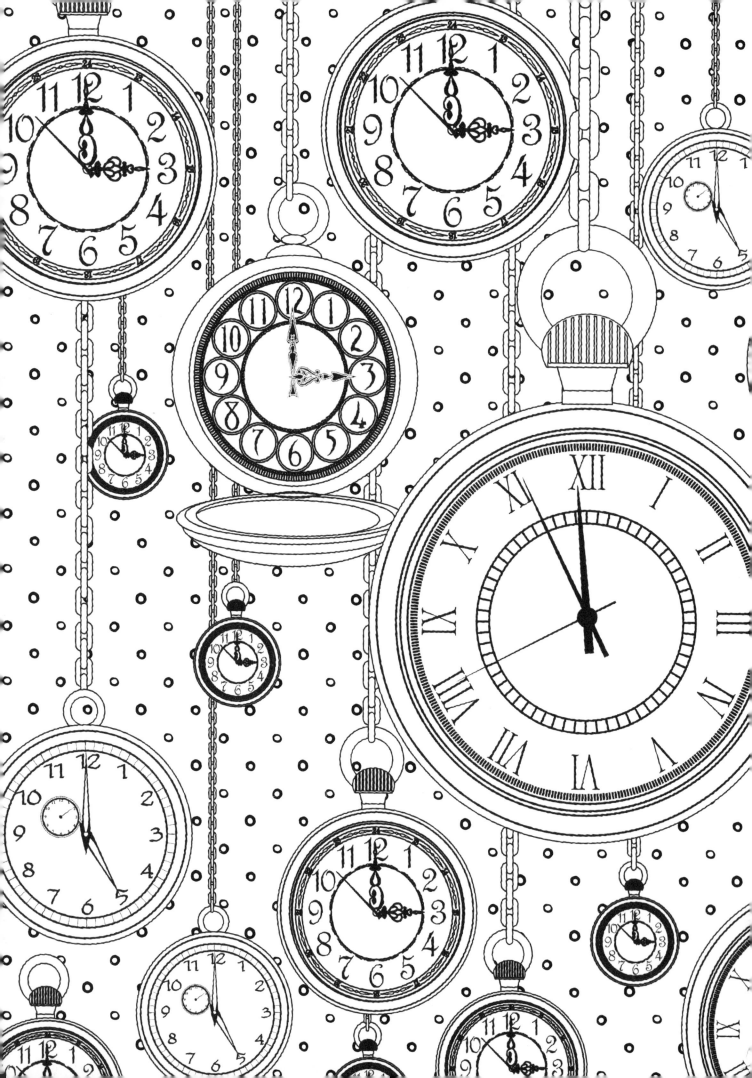

A large rose-tree stood near

the entrance of the garden:

the roses growing on it were white,

but there were three gardeners at it,

busily painting them red.

On this the White Rabbit blew three blasts on the trumpet, and then unrolled the parchment scroll...

...She jumped up in

such a hurry that she tipped

over the jury-box with

the edge of her skirt,

upsetting all the jurymen onto

the heads of the crowd below...

At this the whole pack rose up into the air, and came flying down upon her…

"Let the jury consider their verdict," the King said, for about the twentieth time that day.

They had not gone far before
they saw the Mock Turtle in
the distance, sitting sad and
lonely on a little ledge of rock.

... The wretched Hatter trembled so, that he shook off both his shoes.

The last time she saw them,
they were trying to put the
Dormouse into the teapot.

"You're nothing
but a pack
of cards!"

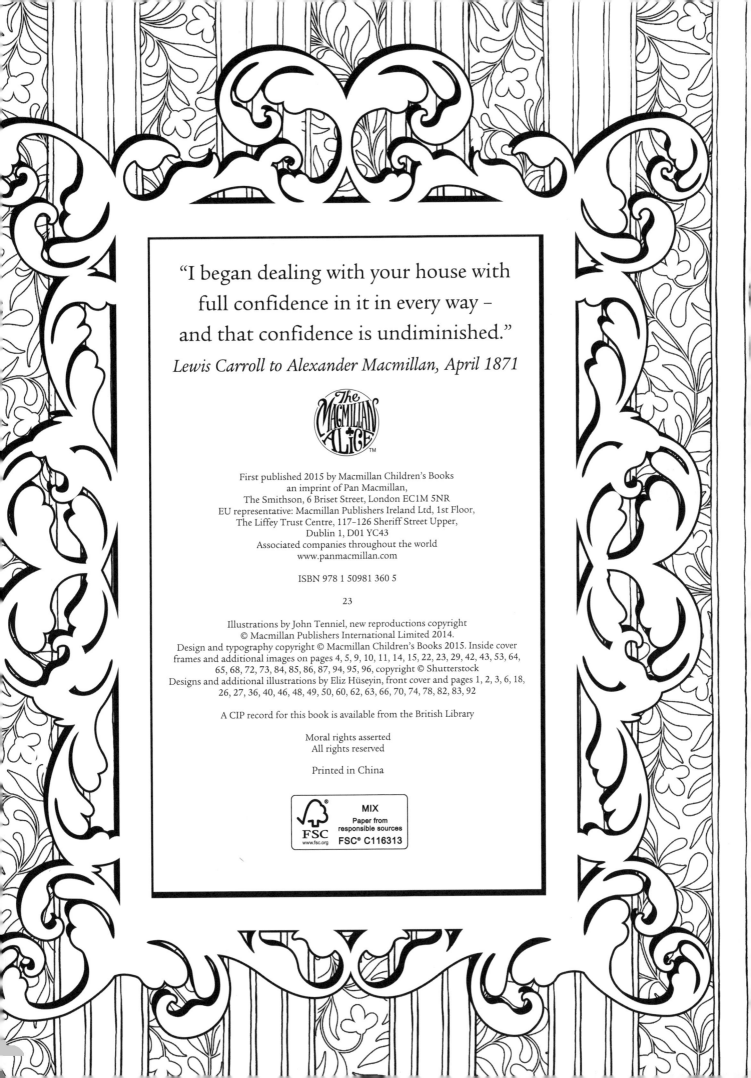

"I began dealing with your house with
full confidence in it in every way –
and that confidence is undiminished."

Lewis Carroll to Alexander Macmillan, April 1871

First published 2015 by Macmillan Children's Books
an imprint of Pan Macmillan,
The Smithson, 6 Briset Street, London EC1M 5NR
EU representative: Macmillan Publishers Ireland Ltd, 1st Floor,
The Liffey Trust Centre, 117–126 Sheriff Street Upper,
Dublin 1, D01 YC43
Associated companies throughout the world
www.panmacmillan.com

ISBN 978 1 50981 360 5

23

Illustrations by John Tenniel, new reproductions copyright
© Macmillan Publishers International Limited 2014.
Design and typography copyright © Macmillan Children's Books 2015. Inside cover
frames and additional images on pages 4, 5, 9, 10, 11, 14, 15, 22, 23, 29, 42, 43, 53, 64,
65, 68, 72, 73, 84, 85, 86, 87, 94, 95, 96, copyright © Shutterstock
Designs and additional illustrations by Eliz Hüseyin, front cover and pages 1, 2, 3, 6, 18,
26, 27, 36, 40, 46, 48, 49, 50, 60, 62, 63, 66, 70, 74, 78, 82, 83, 92

A CIP record for this book is available from the British Library

Printed in China

The story behind the illustrations
for *Alice's Adventures in Wonderland*

Charles Lutwidge Dodgson was a mathematics tutor at Christ Church College Oxford, and better known by his famous pen name, Lewis Carroll. His original story, *Alice's Adventures Underground*, had thirty-seven illustrations drawn by himself. A hand-bound copy was given by Carroll to Alice Liddell, the girl who inspired the story and he also gave copies to his friends, who persuaded him to look for a publisher and illustrator. Carroll met with the publisher Alexander Macmillan in October 1863, and in January 1864 Carroll met with the renowned illustrator John Tenniel. In April Tenniel agreed to illustrate the book, and it was first published in 1865.

John Tenniel was already a well-known artist when Carroll approached him. His cartoons for the magazine *Punch*, where he worked for over fifty years, were famous throughout Britain. He based many of his illustrations on Carroll's original drawings, but in his skilled hands, the characters of Wonderland came to life in an unforgettable way.

Printing Tenniel's images involved careful preparation – the drawings, originally done on paper, had to be carved into woodblocks by wood engravers. The woodblocks were then used to create metal electrotypes that would be used on the printing press. The original woodblocks are now held in the British Library.

John Tenniel's illustrations for *Alice's Adventures in Wonderland* were originally printed in black line, but as the book grew in popularity Lewis Carroll was keen to widen its appeal to include younger children. In 1889 he and Tenniel collaborated with Macmillan to create the first colour edition, *The Nursery Alice*. Tenniel redrew Alice, giving her a yellow dress, and blue bows on her apron and in her hair.

In 1903, Macmillan published *The Little Folks' Edition*, the first colour edition of Alice available at a pocket-money price. In this book Alice has a blue dress in the first edition and a red dress in the second.

Then in 1911 Macmillan published a new version of Alice with selected illustrations coloured by renowned watercolour artist Harry Theaker (1873-1954). This new image of Alice, wearing a blue dress and stripy stockings is the one most recognized as the iconic Alice. In 1995 Macmillan commissioned the artist Diz Wallis to create coloured versions of the rest of Tenniel's original artwork, following the classic colours established by Theaker.